introducing...

Beats Fills
and
Solos for Drums

by
Steve Shier

Acknowledgements
Cover: Phil Martin
Thanks to Jim Leftley for notation assistance.

Distributed by

AUSTRALIA
Koala Publications Pty. Ltd.
37 Orsmond Street,
Hindmarsh 5007
South Australia
Ph: (08) 346 5366
Fax: 61-8-340 9040

USA
Koala Publications Inc.
3001 Redhill Ave.
Bldg 2#109
Costa Mesa
CA. 92626
Ph: (714) 546 2743
Fax: 1-714-546 2749

U.K. and Europe
Music Exchange,
Mail Order Dept,
Claverton Rd, Wythenshawe,
Manchester M23 9NE
Ph: (061) 946 1234
Fax: (061) 946 1195

Order Code KP-IBF

ISBN 1 875726 05 5

Contents

Introduction 4

SECTION 1
    Lets Rock
    Lesson 1. Rock Beats 6
    Lesson 2. Rock Fills 12
    Lesson 3. Rock Solos 17
    Solo No. 1. 'Sixteen Boulders' 18
    Solo No. 2. 'Sticks and Stones' 20

SECTION 2
    Got The Blues
    Lesson 4. Blues Beats 23
    Lesson 5. Blues Fills 28
    Solo No. 3. 'Tom Cat Stew' 32
    Solo No. 4. 'Double Trouble Blues' 34

SECTION 3
    Funk Out
    Lesson 6. Funk Beats 37
    Lesson 7. Funk Fills 42
    Solo No. 5. 'Funky Junk' 46
    Solo No. 6 'Gettin' Down' 48

SECTION 4
    All That Jazz
    Lesson 8. Jazz Beats 51
    Lesson 9. Jazz Fills 55
    Solo No. 7. 'Swing Time Baby' 58
    Solo No. 8. 'Keepin' Time' 60
    Solo No. 9. 'Jigsaw Jazz' 62

Summary 64

Introduction

This book is designed to help the drummer master beats , fills and solos in a range of different styles.

Each section works through progressively from simple beats and fills, suitable for the beginner, right through to the professional players standard.

This book is a must for any drummer who is playing in a band, or who would like to become a professional player.

Every section in this book contains beats and fills that you can use effectively in every-day playing. All the notation is big and very easy to read, however it is important touse the **'Beats Fills and Solos' C.D.**

For an introduction to basic drumming for the beginner see, *"Introducing Drums"* by Steve Shier.
For great triplet and paradiddle studies see, *"Introducing All Around The Drums"* by Steve Shier.
Please note that it is important to keep your drum kit sounding great. For correct tuning methods see, *"Introducing How To Tune The Drums"* also by Steve Shier.

Notation

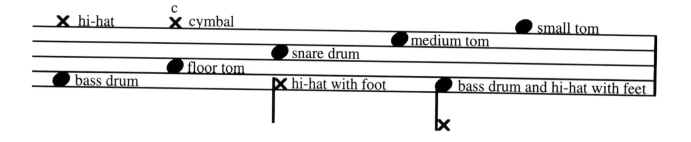

Section One

Lets Rock

Lesson One

Rock Beats Between The Hi-Hat, The Snare Drum and The Bass Drum, With Quarter Notes, Eighth Notes and Sixteenth Notes

Remember to **count** out loud while you
play along with these Rock beats.
Listen to this example on the
" BEATS FILLS AND SOLOS " C.D.

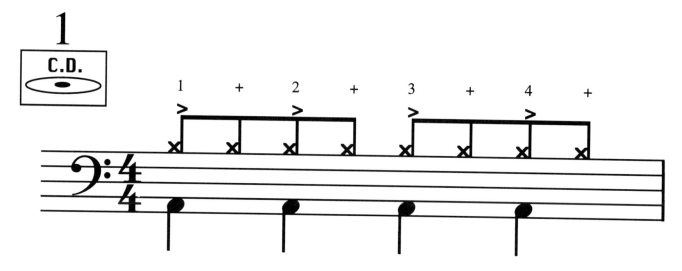

Play each of the following beats through **four** times
with the "BEATS FILLS AND SOLOS" C.D.
Remember to **count** out loud while you play.

7

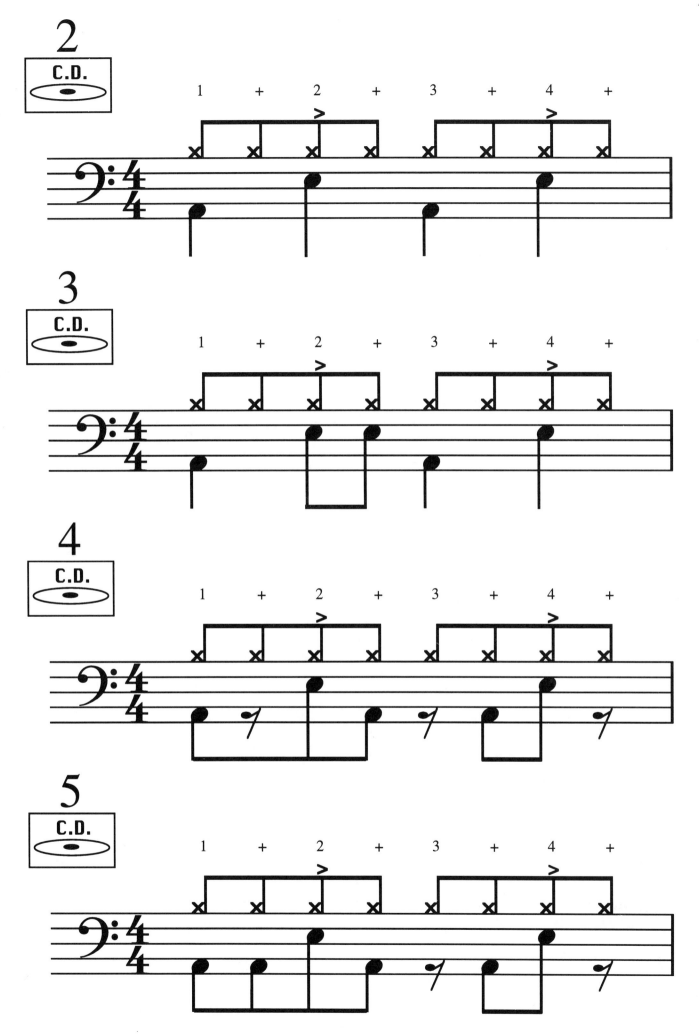

8

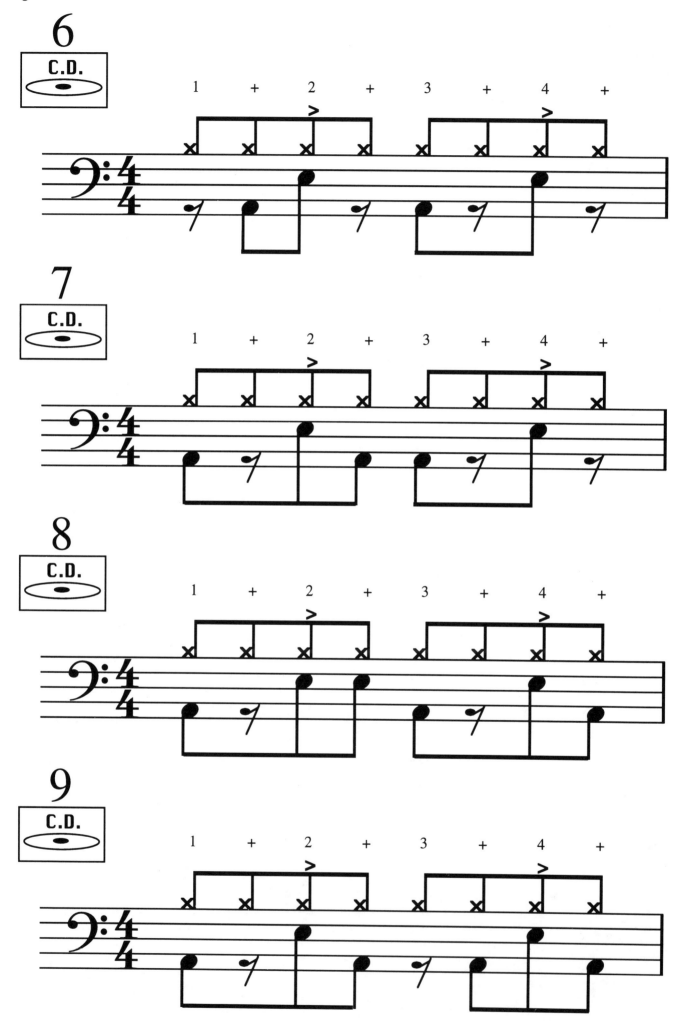

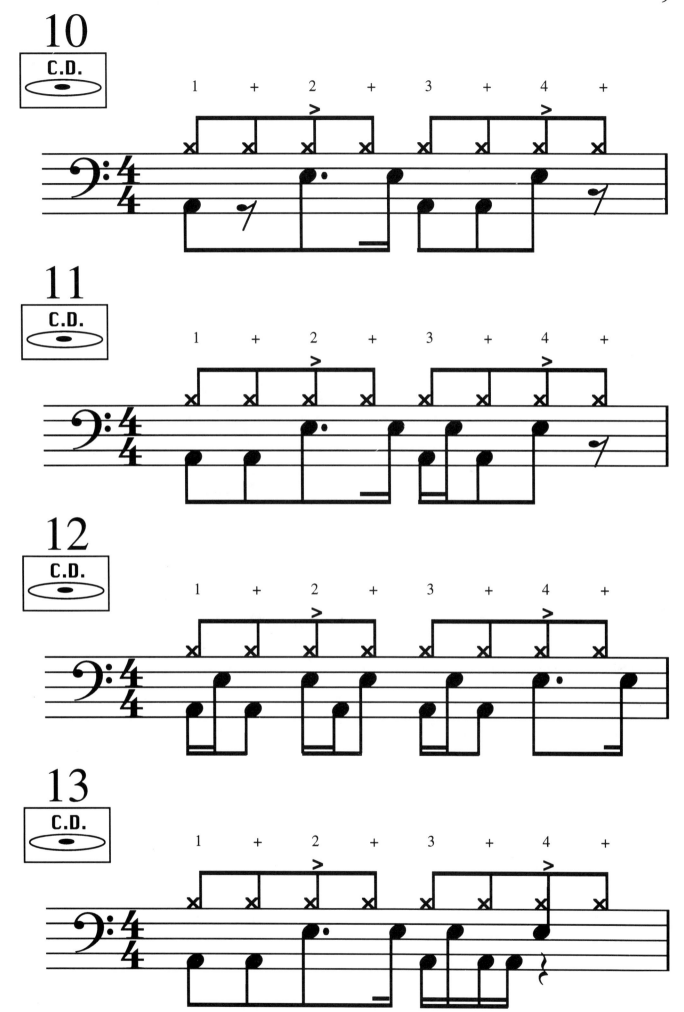

10

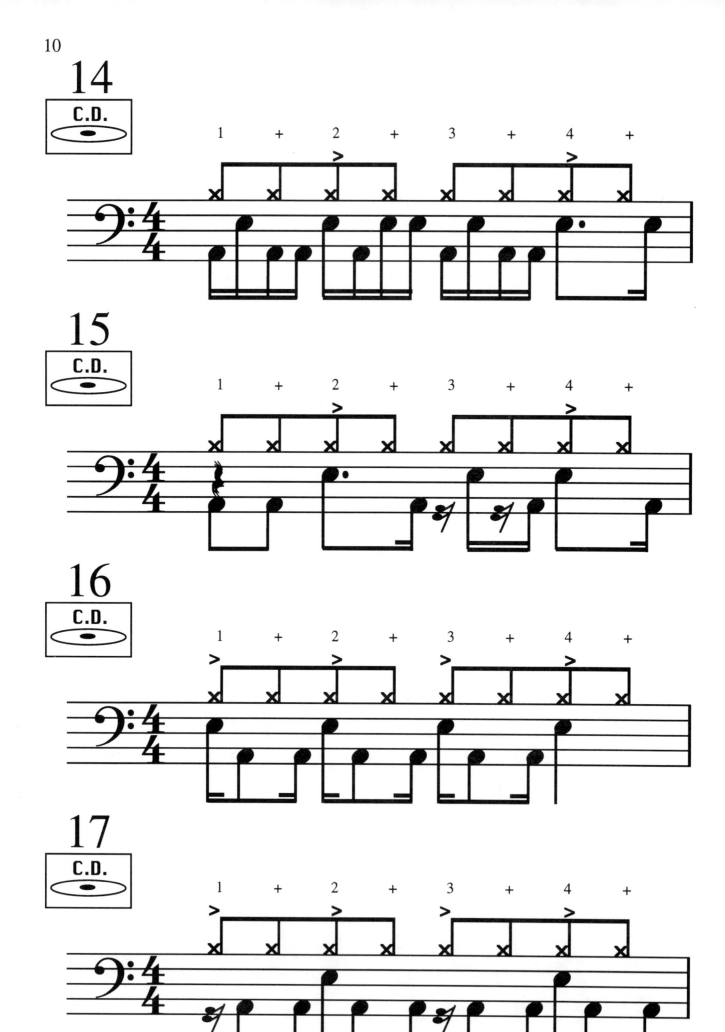

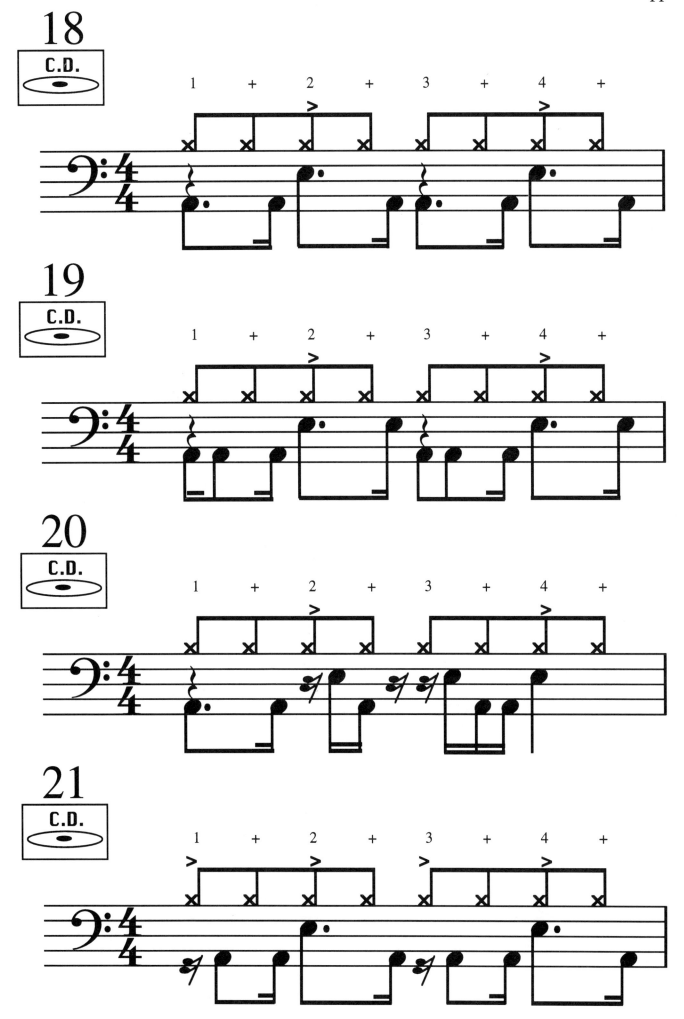

Lesson Two

Rock Fills Around
The Drum Kit With Quarter Notes,
Eighth Notes and Sixteenth Notes

To play these fills effectively, you will need to master the **" FLAM ."**
A flam is when you hit the drum with both sticks almost at the same time.
The stick that strikes the drum **FIRST,** must be a **QUIET** hit and is called a **GRACE** note.
The stick that strikes the drum **LAST,** must be a **LOUDER** hit and is called the **PRINCIPAL**
note. These two hits must be close enough together that they create one sound. Play each of
these examples through eight times with the "BEATS FILLS AND SOLOS" C.D.

" The FLAM "

Example of Right Hand
FLAM

Example of Left Hand
FLAM

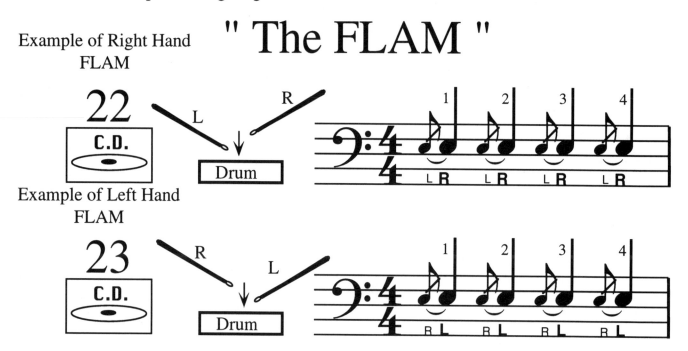

Example of Alternating
Right and Left FLAMS
with bass drum inbetween

Play each of the following Fills through **four** times
with the "BEATS FILLS AND SOLOS" C.D.

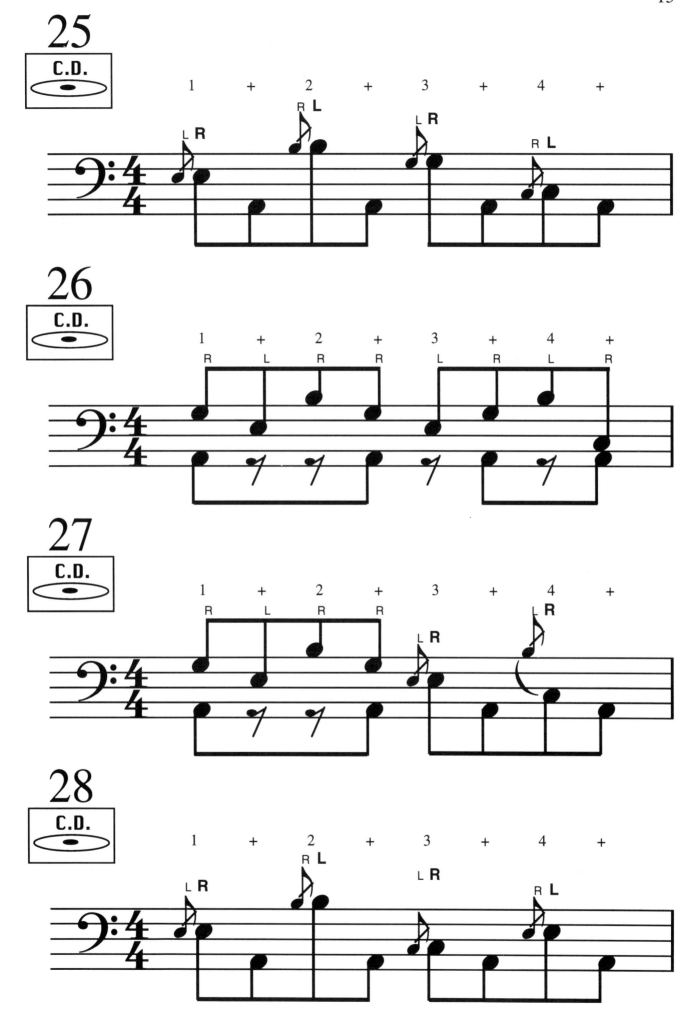

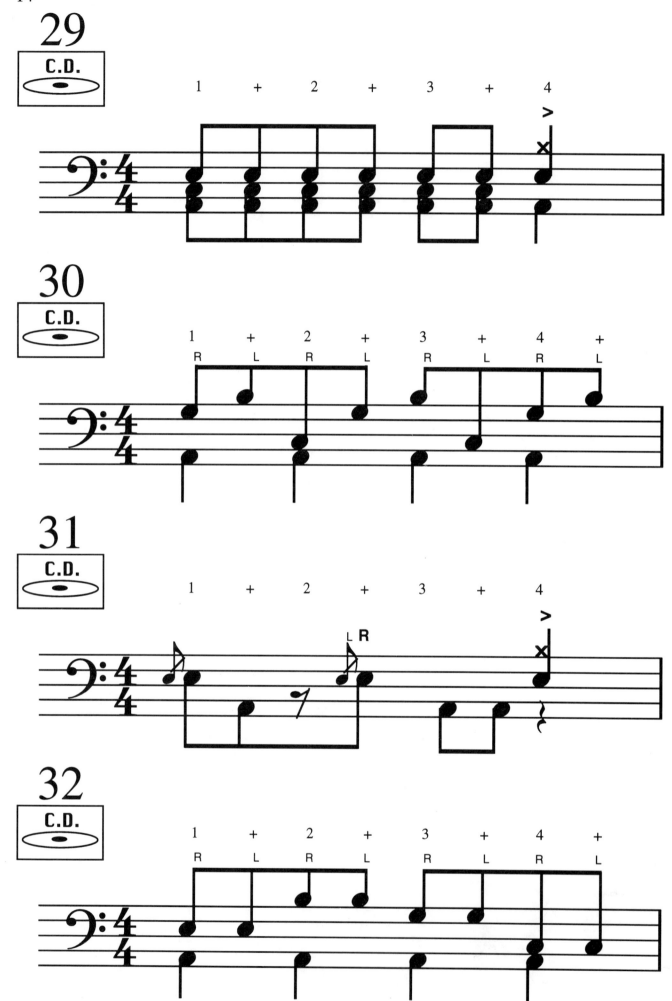

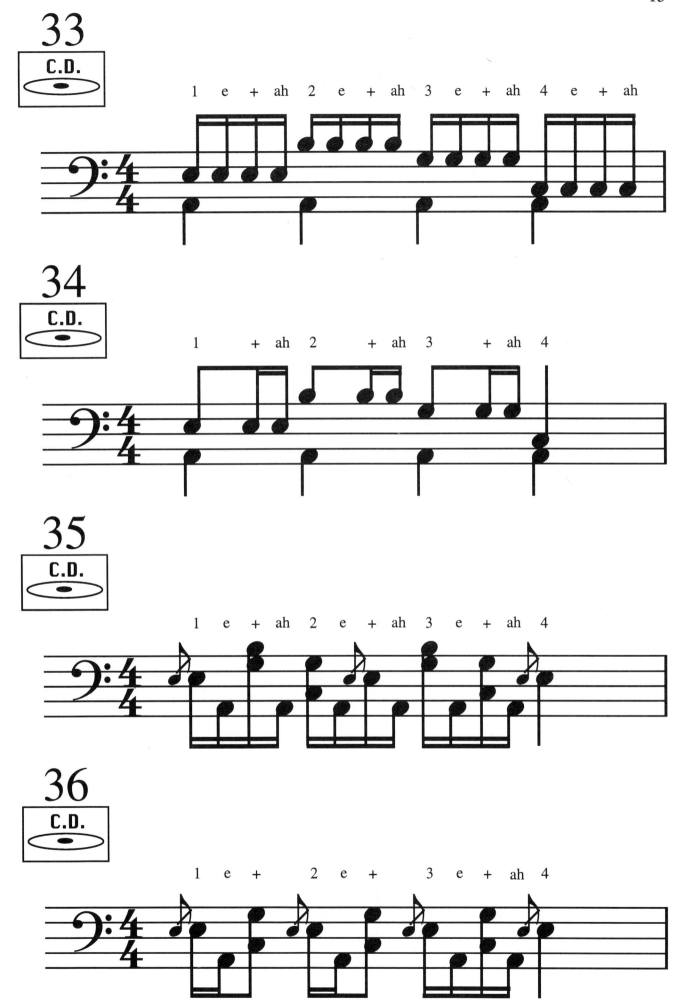

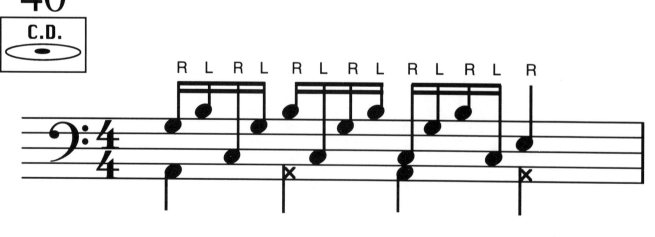

Lesson Three

Lesson Three consists of two sixteen bar Rock Solos. The first solo, "Sixteen Boulders" uses quarter notes and eighth notes. The second solo, "Sticks and Stones" uses quarter notes, eighth notes and sixteenth notes.

Play each solo through once
with the "BEATS FILLS AND SOLOS" C.D.
Remember to **count** out loud while you play.

Solo No. 1

Sixteen Boulders

This sixteen bar drum solo utilizes beats and fills with quarter notes and eighth notes from lessons 1 and 2. It is more important to place the emphasis on accuracy rather than speed. Try to create a relaxed flowing feel and allow the accents to highlight and colour the solo. Remember to count as you play along with the **"Beats Fills and Solos" C.D.**

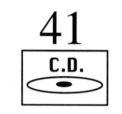

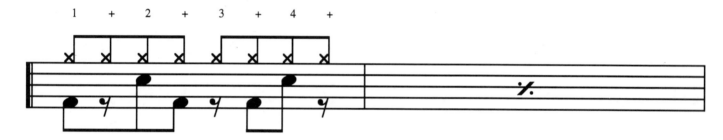

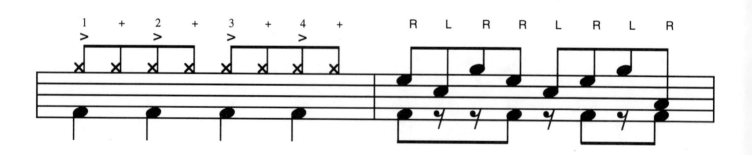

Solo No. 2

Sticks and Stones

This sixteen bar drum solo utilizes beats and fills with quarter notes, eighth notes and sixteenth notes from lessons 1 and 2. It is more important to place the emphasis on accuracy rather than speed. Allow the accents to highlight and colour the solo. Remember to count as you play along with the **"Beats Fills and Solos" C.D.**

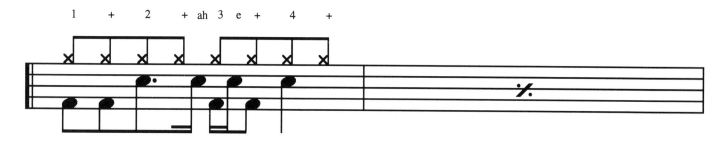

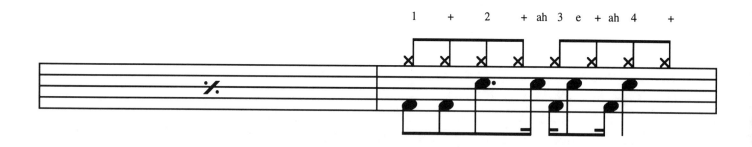

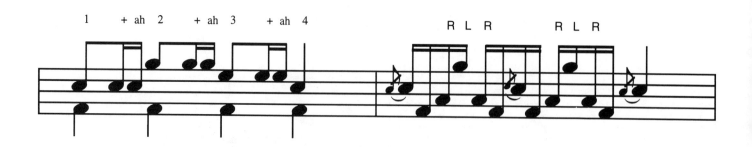

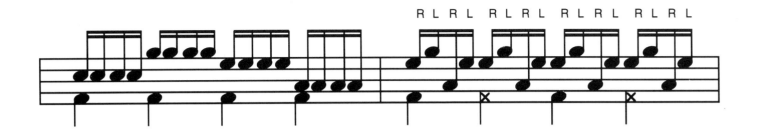

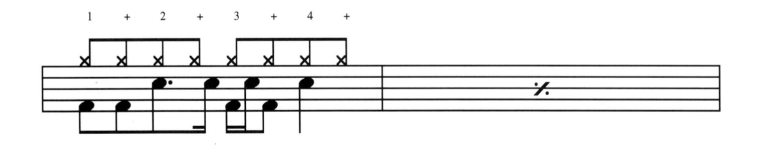

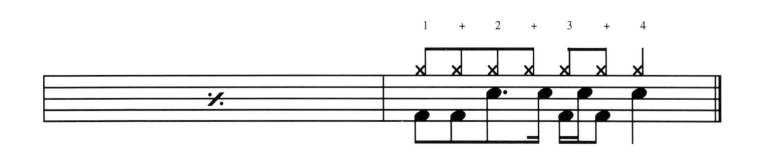

Section Two

Got The Blues

Lesson Four

Blues Beats Between The Ride Cymbal or The Hi-Hat, The Snare Drum and The Bass Drum, With Quarter Notes, Eighth Notes and Sixteenth Notes

Remember to **count** out loud while you
play along with these Blues beats.
Listen to this example on the
" BEATS FILLS AND SOLOS " C.D.

43
C.D.

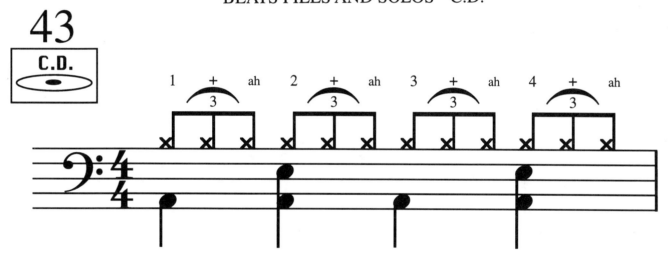

Play each of the following beats through **four** times
with the "BEATS FILLS AND SOLOS" C.D.
Remember to **count** out loud while you play.

24

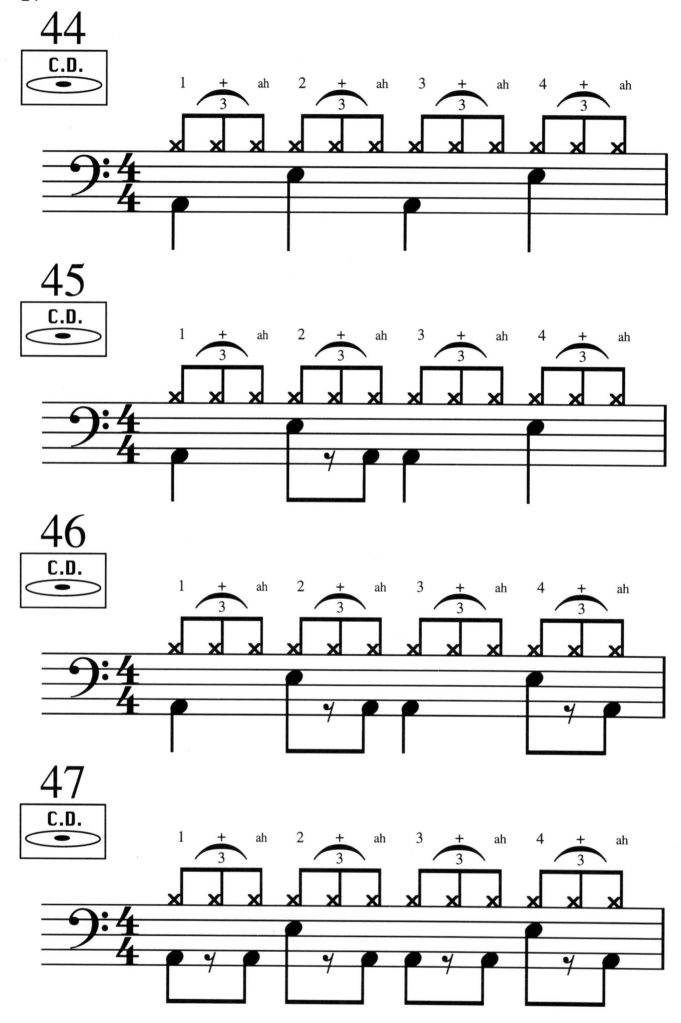

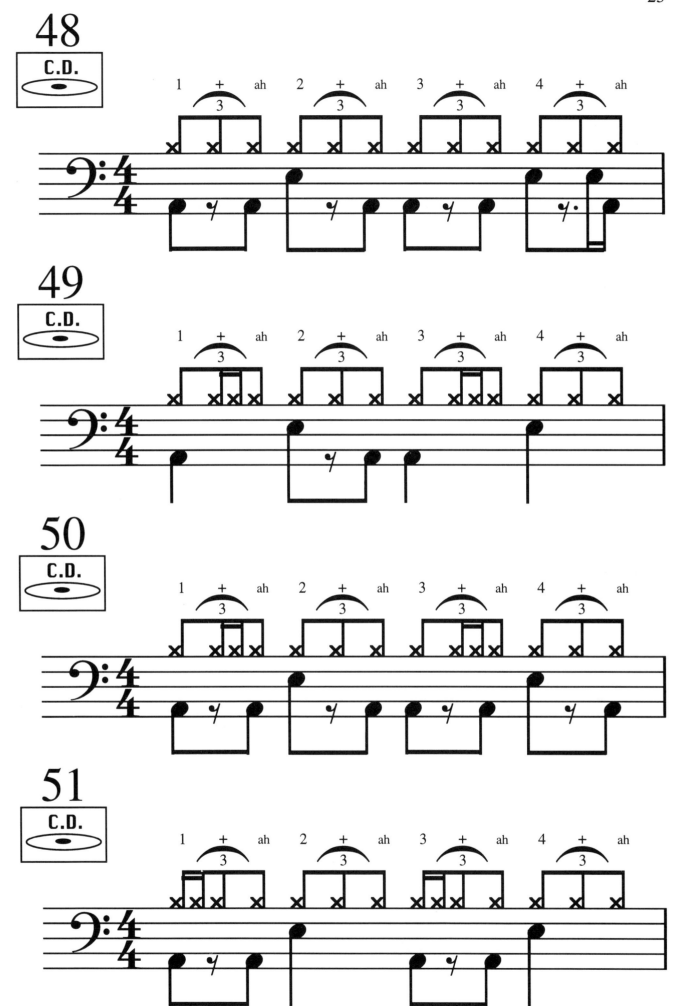

26

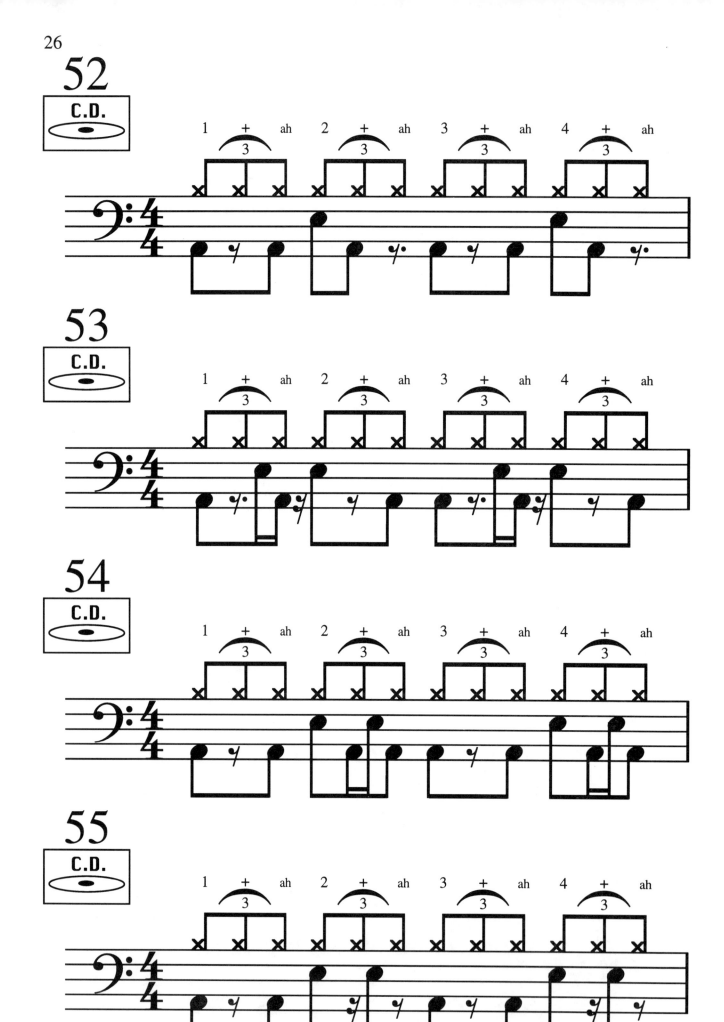

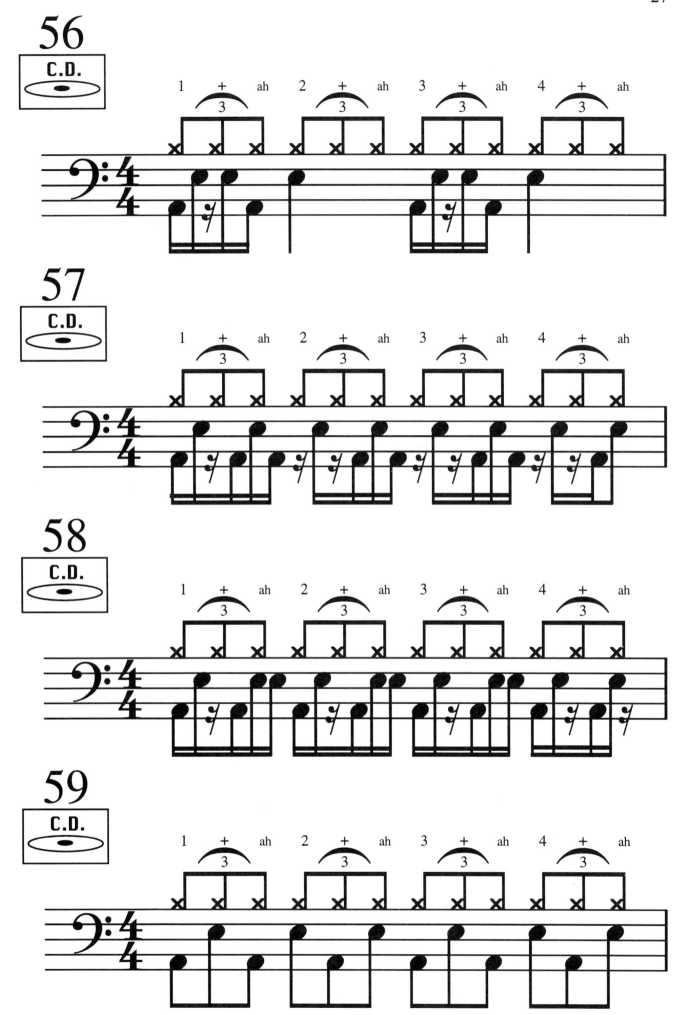

Lesson Five

Blues Fills Around
The Drums With Quarter Notes,
Eighth Notes and Sixteenth Notes

Remember to **count** out loud while you
play along with these Blues Fills.
Listen to this example on the
" BEATS FILLS AND SOLOS " C.D.

60

C.D.

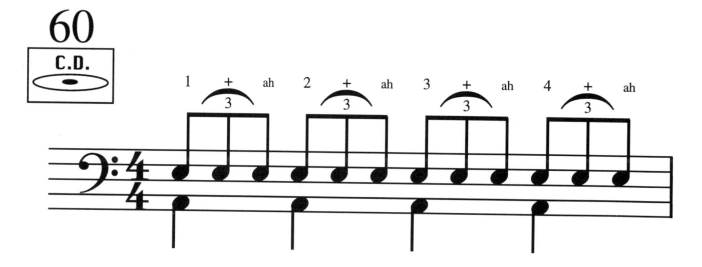

Play each of the following Fills through **four** times
with the"BEATS FILLS AND SOLOS"C.D.
Remember to **count** out loud while you play.

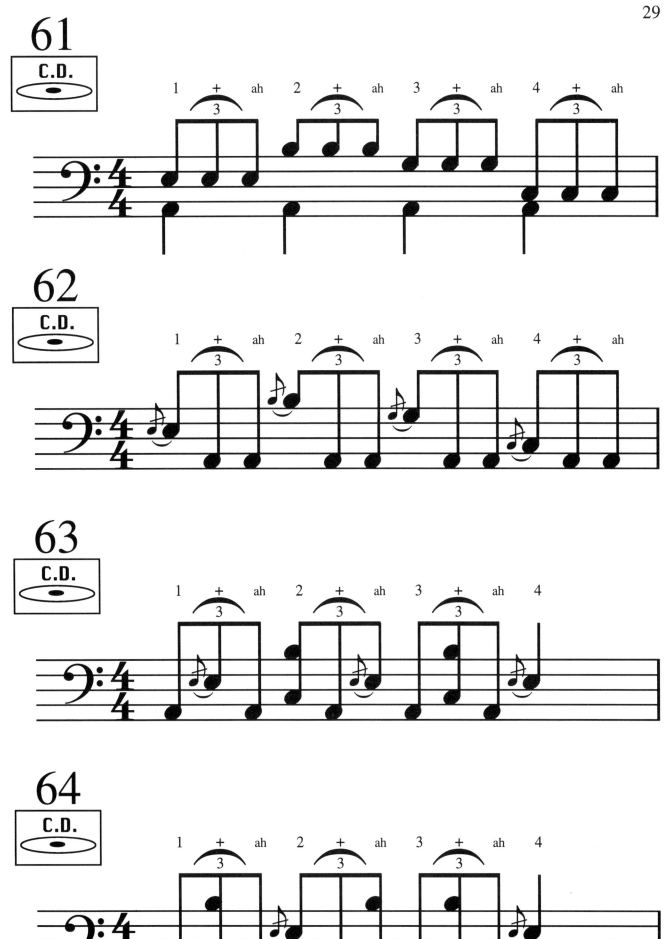

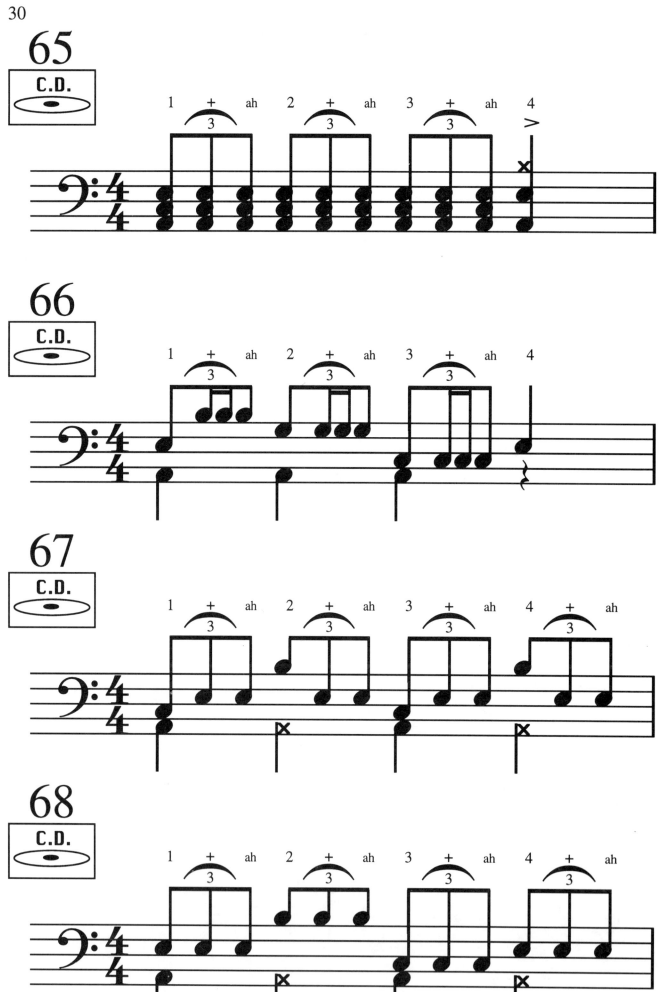

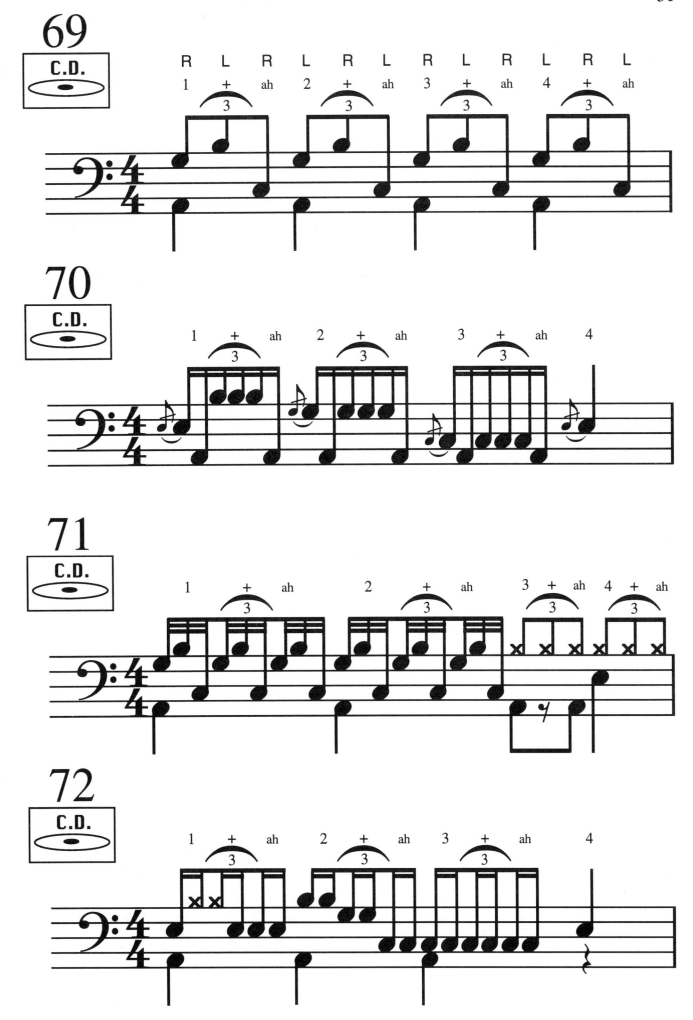

Solo No. 3

Tom Cat Stew

This sixteen bar drum solo utilizes beats and fills with quarter notes, eighth and sixteenth notes from lessons 4 and 5. It is more important to place the emphasis on accuracy rather than speed. Try to create a relaxed flowing feel and allow the accents to highlight and colour the solo. Remember to count as you play along with the **"Beats Fills and Solos" C.D.**

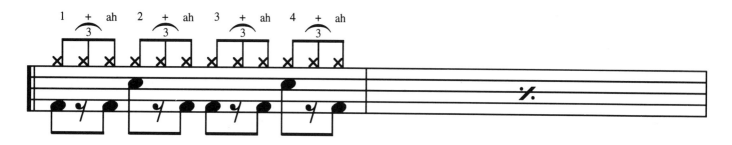

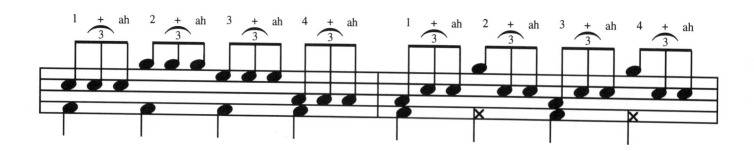

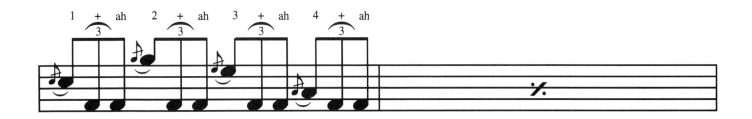

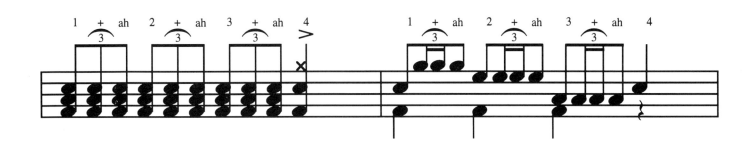

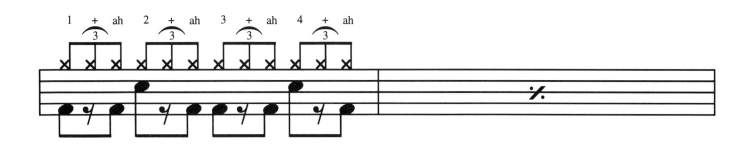

Solo No. 4

Double Trouble Blues

This sixteen bar drum solo utilizes beats and fills with quarter notes, eighth and sixteenth notes from lessons 4 and 5. It is more important to place the emphasis on accuracy rather than speed. Try to create a relaxed flowing feel and allow the accents to highlight and colour the solo. Remember to count as you play along with the **"Beats Fills and Solos" C.D.**

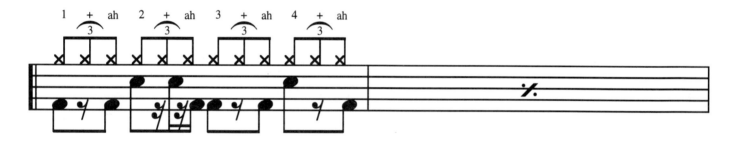

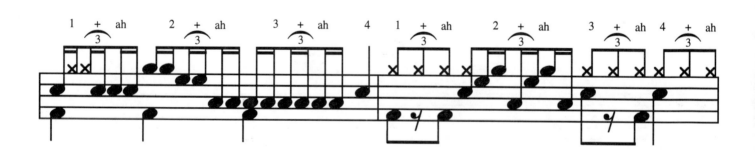

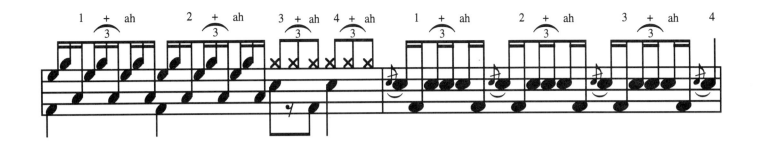

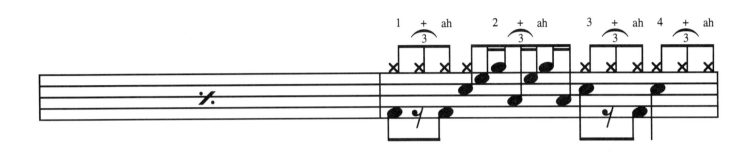

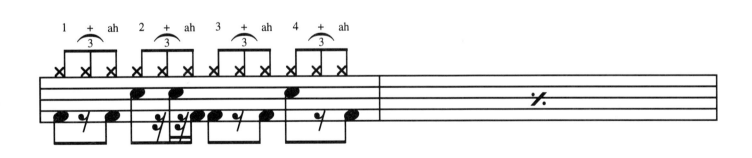

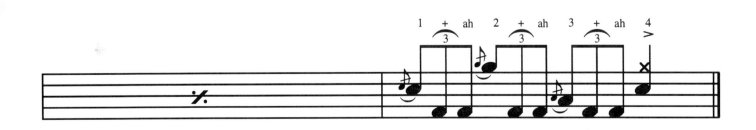

Section Three

Funk Out !

Lesson Six

Funk Beats Between The Hi-Hat or The Cymbal, The Snare Drum and The Bass Drum, With Quarter Notes, Eighth Notes and Sixteenth Notes. When a Cymbal Hit is Required, "c" Will Appear Above The Hi-Hat Sign.

Remember to **count** out loud while you
play along with these Funk beats.
Listen to this example on the
" BEATS FILLS AND SOLOS " C.D.

75

C.D.

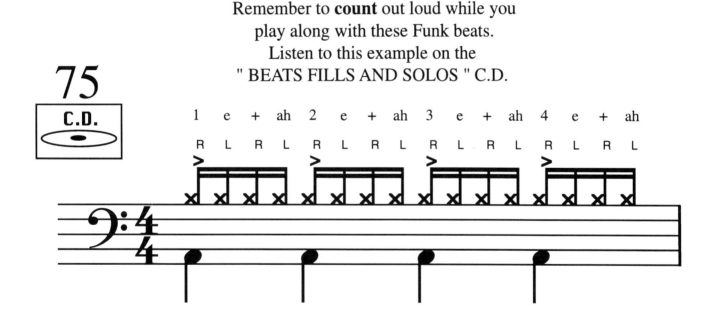

Play each of the following beats through **four** times
with the "BEATS FILLS AND SOLOS" C.D.
Remember to **count** out loud while you play.

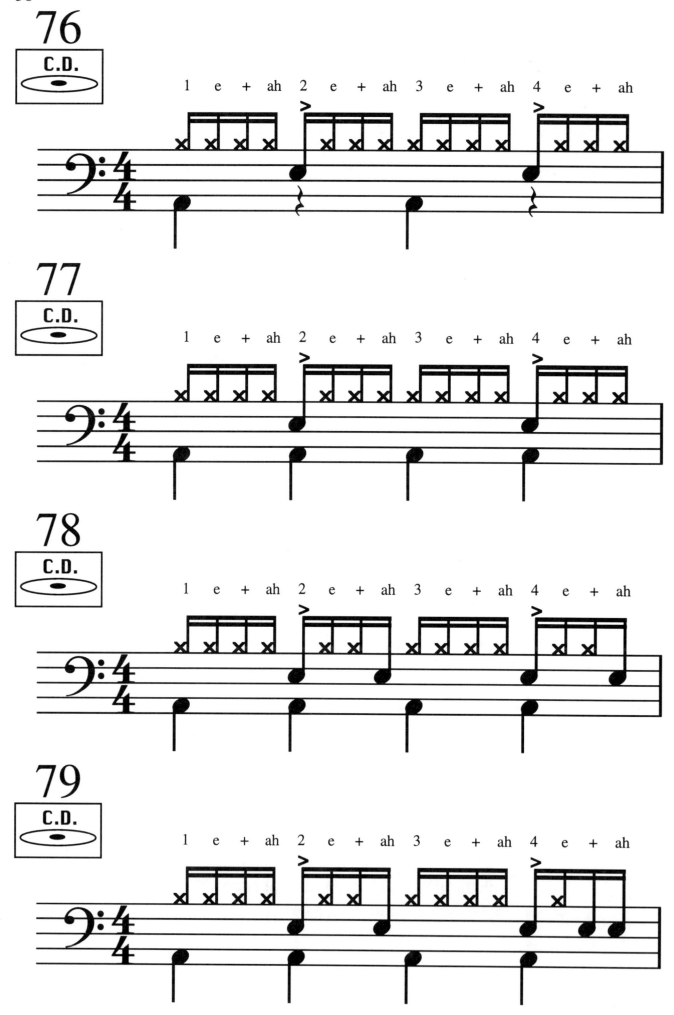

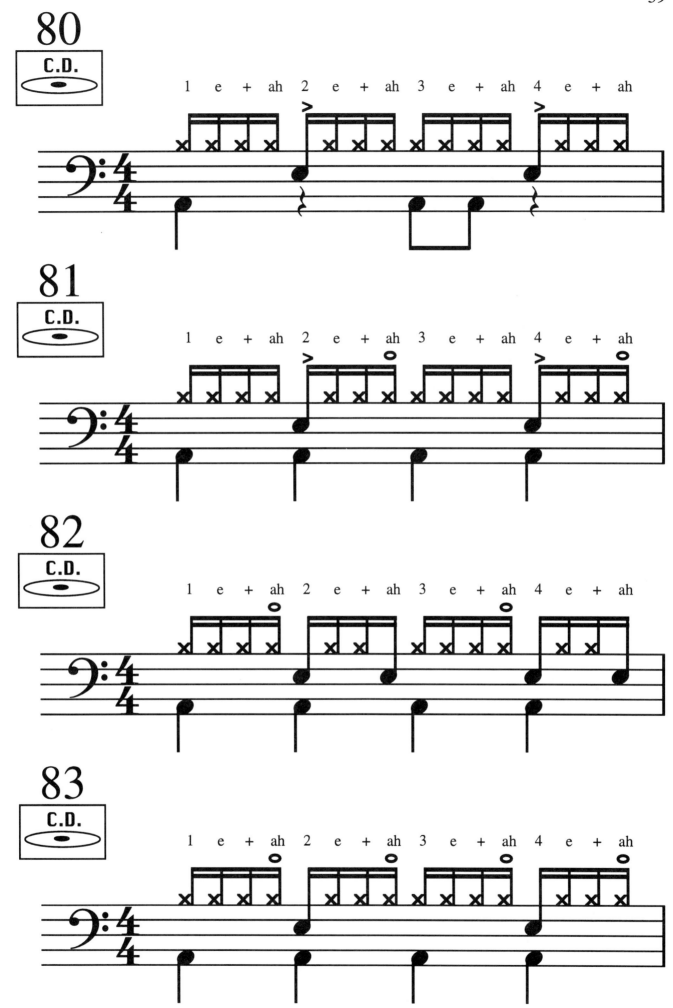

40

84

85

86

87

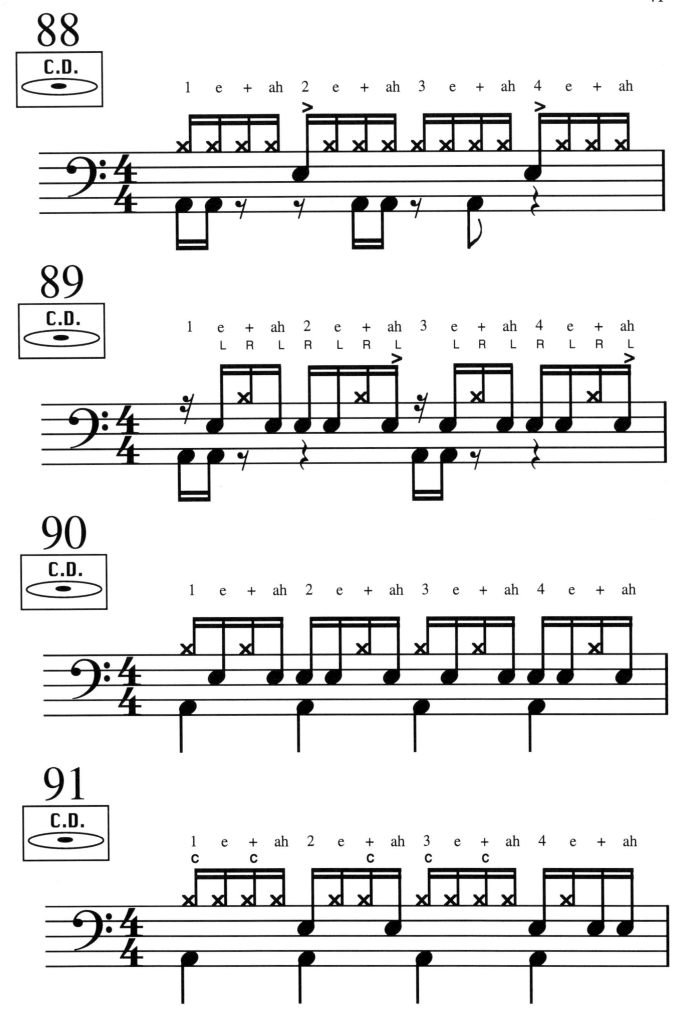

Lesson Seven

Funk Fills Around
The Drums With Quarter Notes,
Eighth Notes and Sixteenth Notes

Remember to **count** out loud while you
play along with these Funk Fills.
Listen to this example on the
" BEATS FILLS AND SOLOS " C.D.

92

C.D.

Play each of the following Fills through **four** times
with the"BEATS FILLS AND SOLOS"C.D.
Remember to **count** out loud while you play.

43

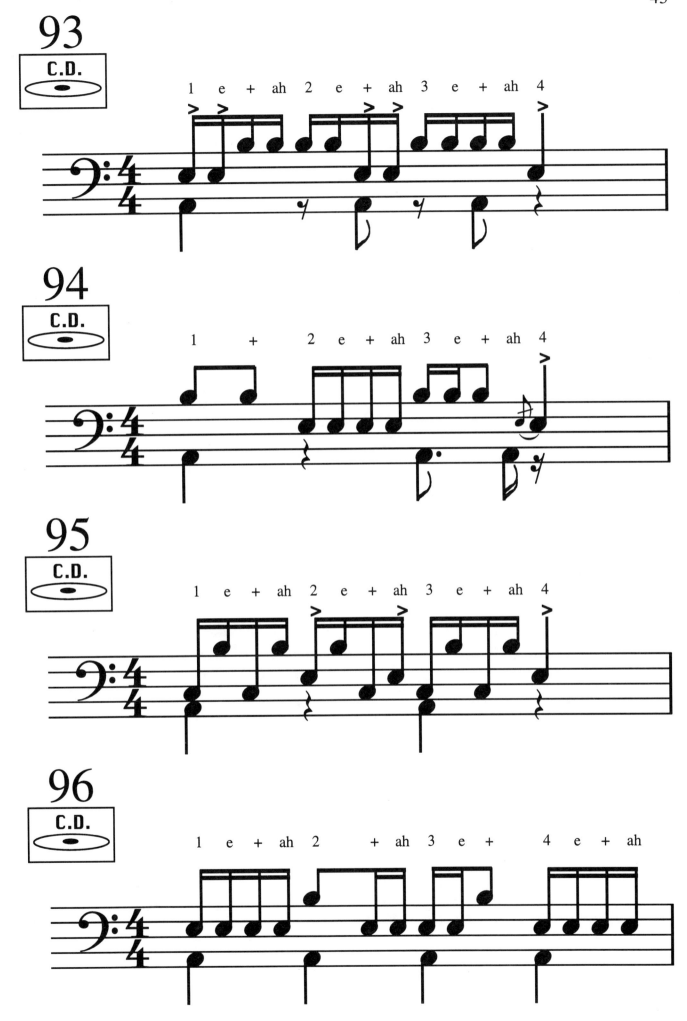

97

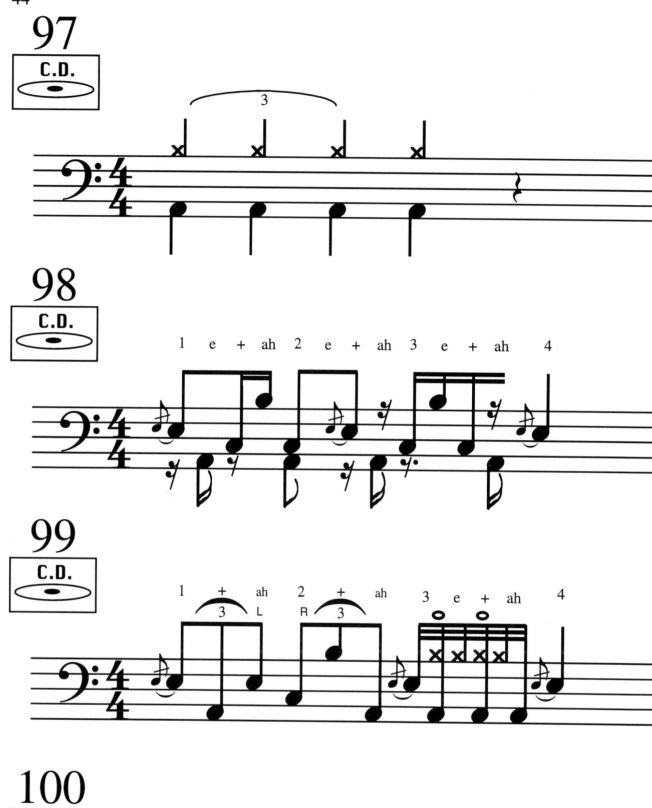

98

99

100

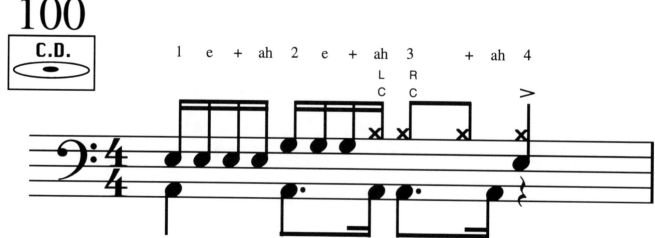

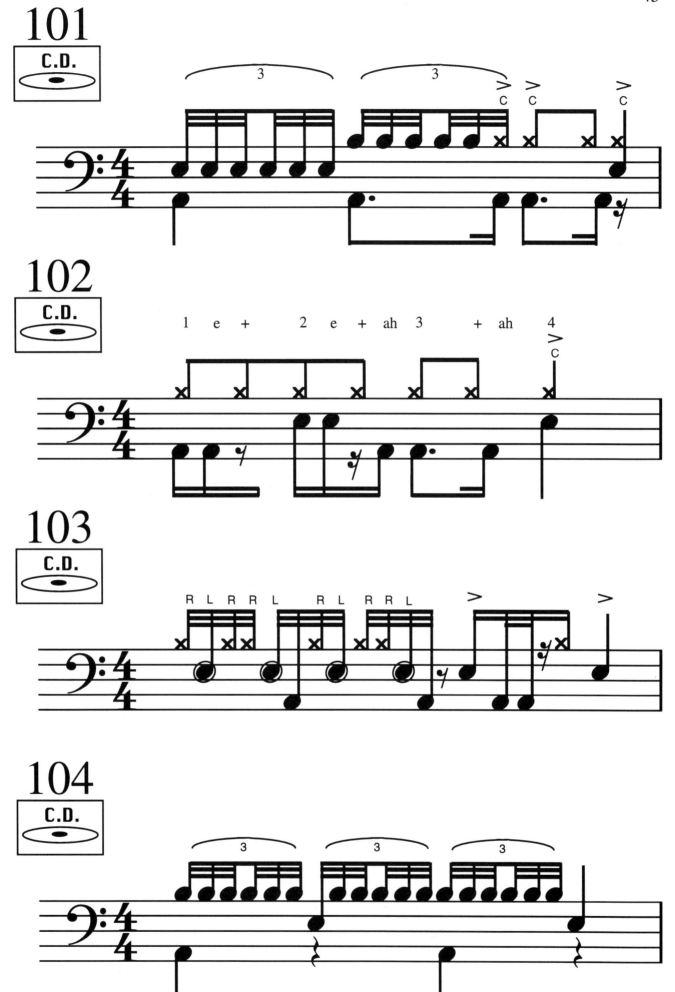

Solo No. 5

Funky Junk

This sixteen bar drum solo utilizes beats and fills with quarter notes, eighth and sixteenth notes from lessons 6 and 7. It is more important to place the emphasis on accuracy rather than speed. Try to create a relaxed flowing feel and allow the accents to highlight and colour the solo. Remember to count as you play along with the **"Beats Fills and Solos" C.D.**

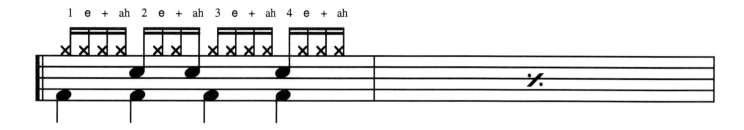

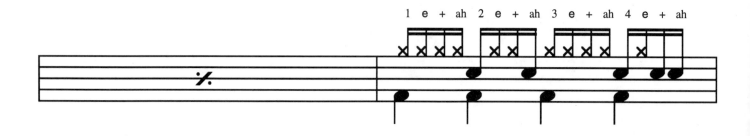

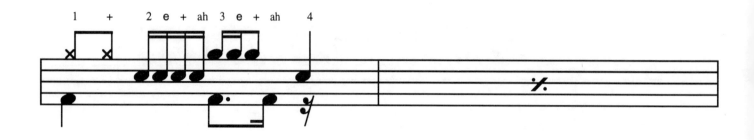

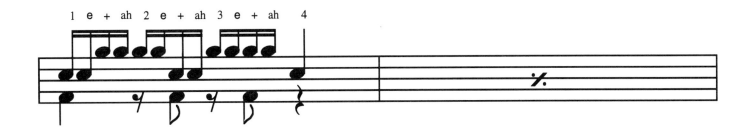

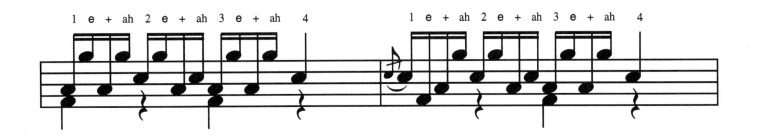

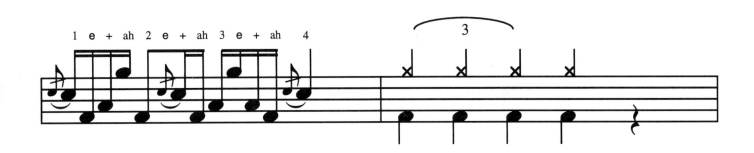

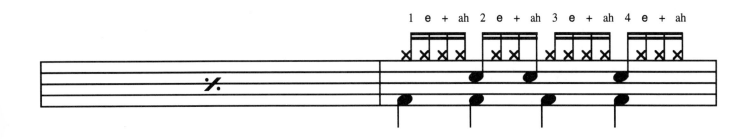

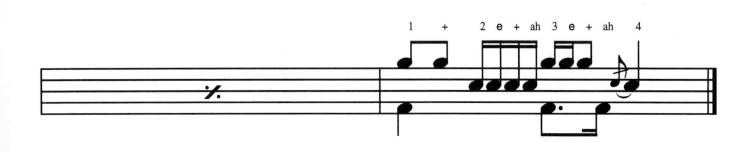

Solo No. 6

Gettin' Down

This sixteen bar drum solo utilizes beats and fills with quarter notes, eighths, sixteenths, and other notes from lessons 6 and 7. It is more important to place the emphasis on accuracy rather than speed. Try to create a relaxed flowing feel and allow the accents to highlight and colour the solo. Remember to count as you play along with the **"Beats Fills and Solos" C.D.**

106

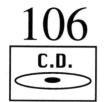

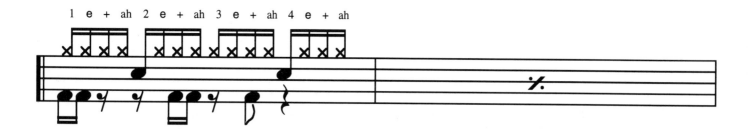

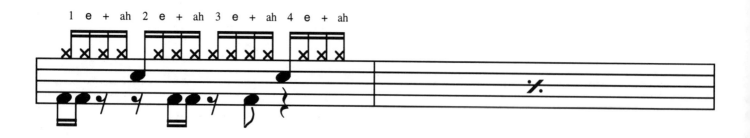

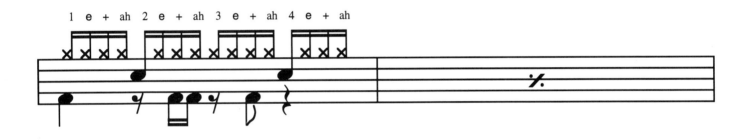

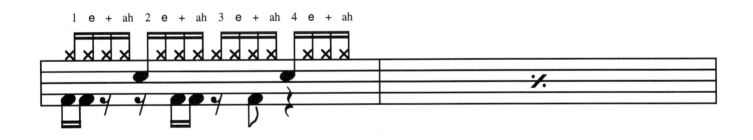

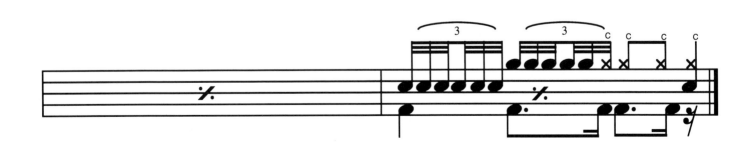

Section Four

All That Jazz

Lesson Eight

Jazz Beats Between The Ride Cymbal, The Snare Drum and The Bass Drum, With Quarter Notes, Eighth Notes and Sixteenth Notes.

Remember to **count** out loud while you
play along with these Jazz beats.
Listen to this example on the
" BEATS FILLS AND SOLOS " C.D.

107

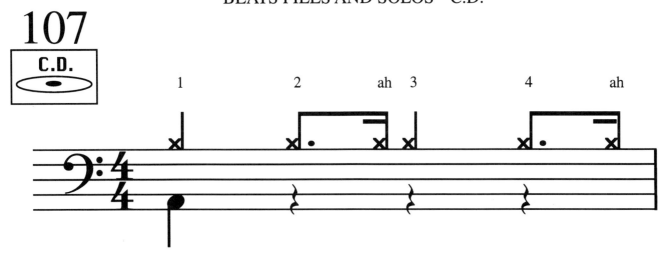

Play each of the following beats through **four** times
with the "BEATS FILLS AND SOLOS" C.D.
Remember to **count** out loud while you play.

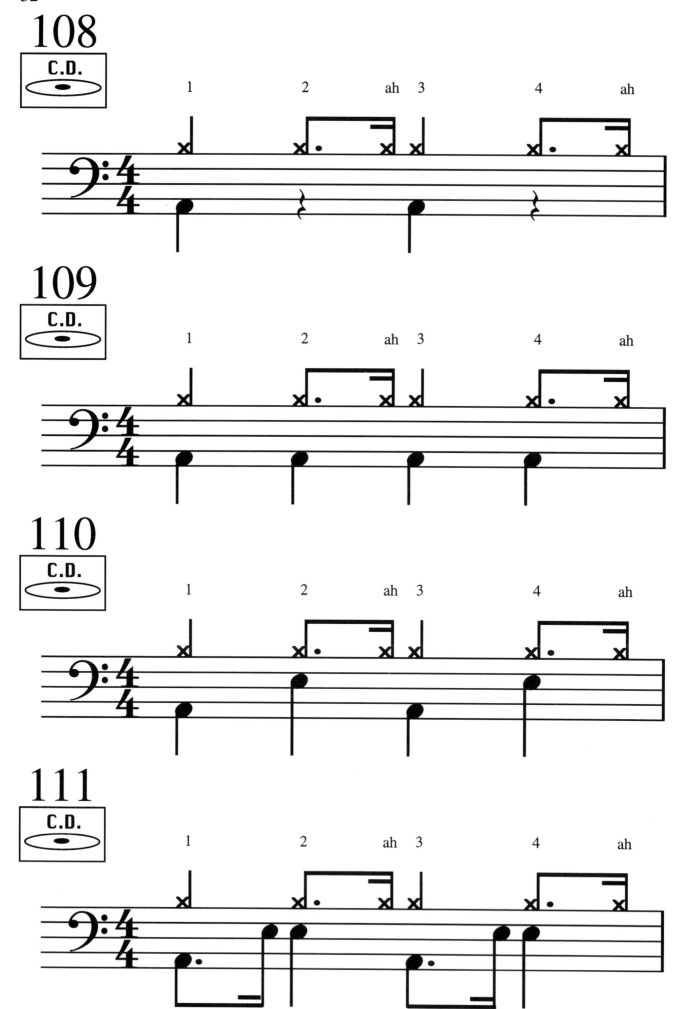

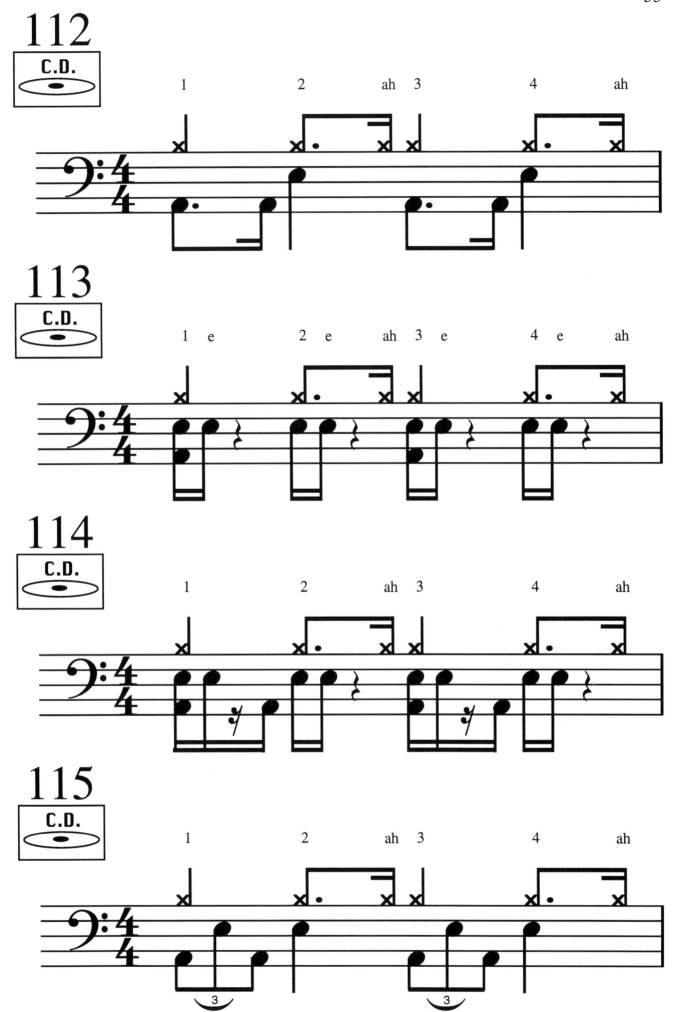

54

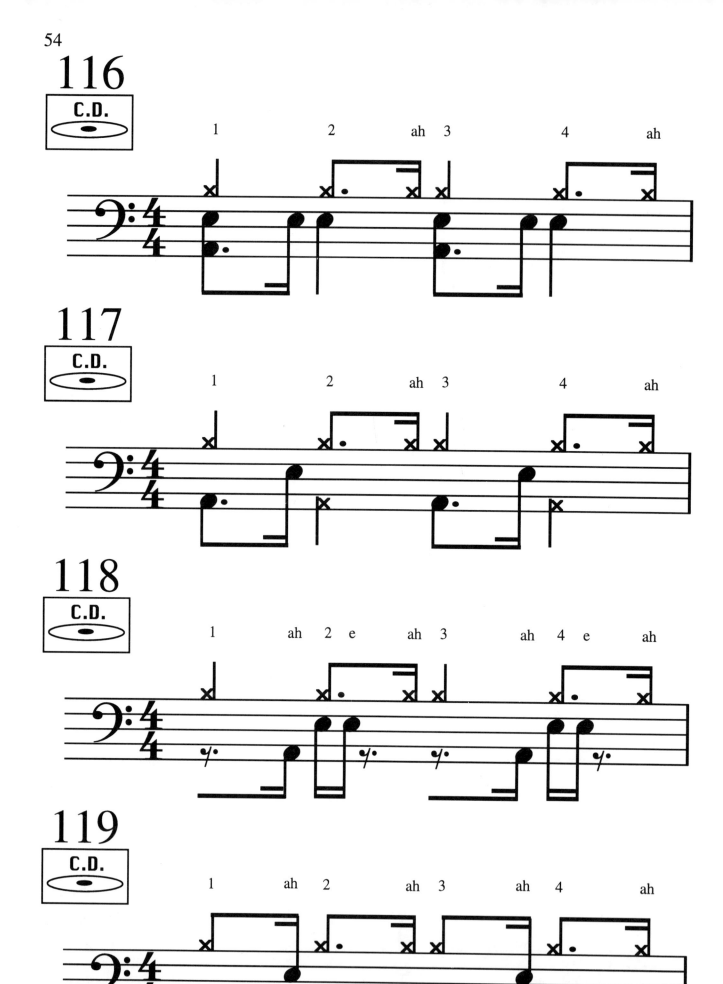

Lesson Nine

Jazz Fills Between The Ride Cymbal,The Snare Drum and The Bass Drum, With Quarter Notes,Eighth Notes and Sixteenth Notes.

Remember to **count** out loud while you
play along with these Jazz Fills.
Listen to this example on the
" BEATS FILLS AND SOLOS " C.D.

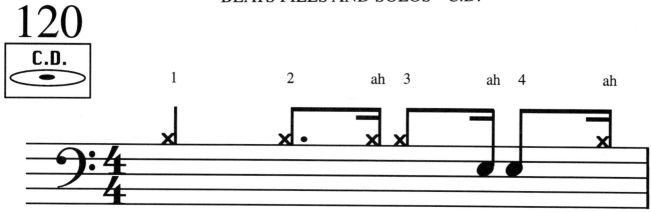

Play each of the following beats through **four** times
with the"BEATS FILLS AND SOLOS"C.D.
Remember to **count** out loud while you play.

56

121

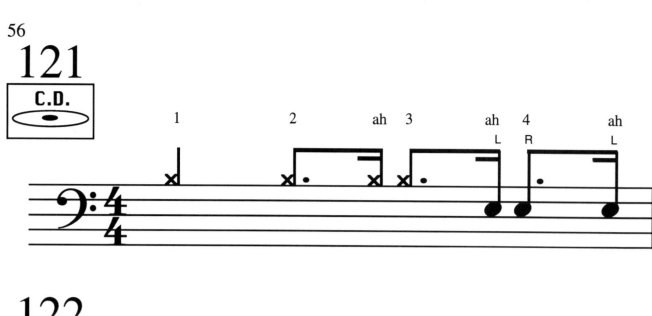

122

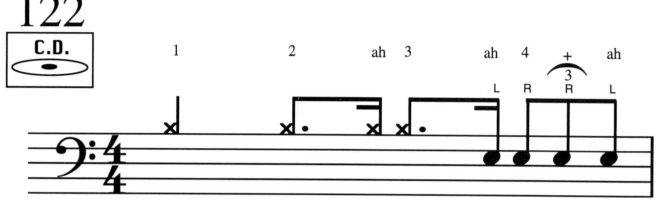

123

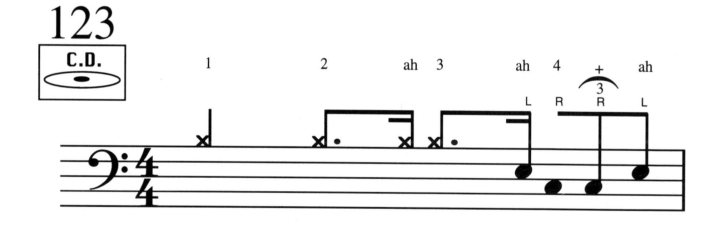

124

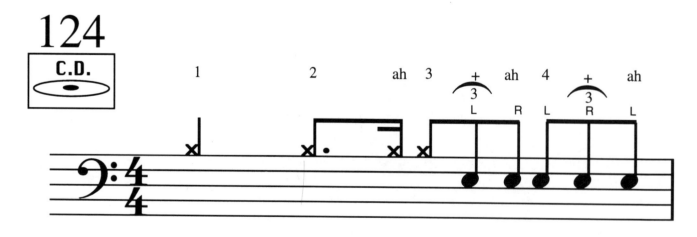

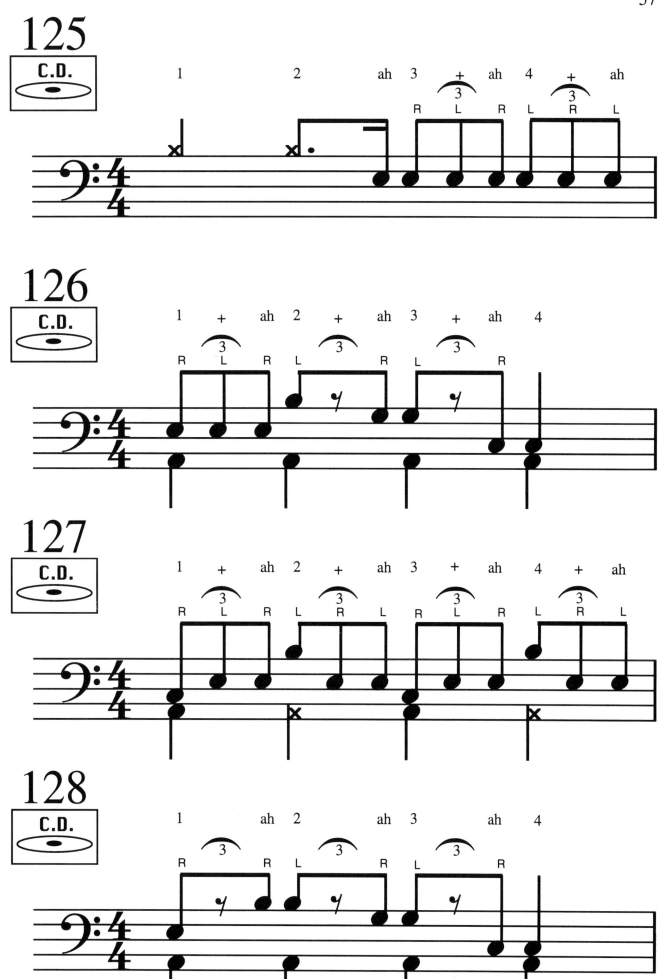

Solo No. 7

Swing Time Baby

This sixteen bar drum solo utilizes beats and fills with quarter notes, eighth and sixteenth notes from lessons 8 and 9. It is more important to place the emphasis on accuracy rather than speed. Try to create a relaxed flowing feel and allow the accents to highlight and colour the solo. Remember to count as you play along with the **"Beats Fills and Solos"** C.D.

129
C.D.

Solo No. 8

Keepin' Time

This sixteen bar drum solo utilizes beats and fills with quarter notes, eighth and sixteenth notes from lessons 8 and 9. It is more important to place the emphasis on accuracy rather than speed. Try to create a relaxed flowing feel and allow the accents to highlight and colour the solo. Remember to count as you play along with the **"Beats Fills and Solos" C.D.**

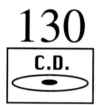

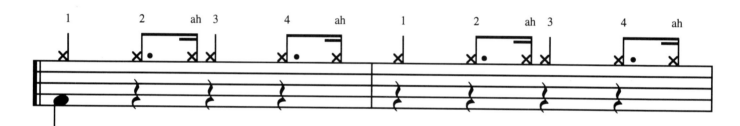

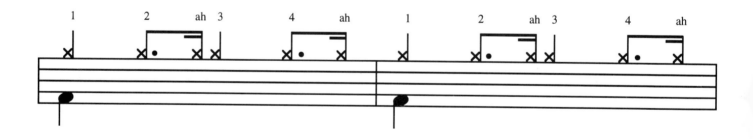

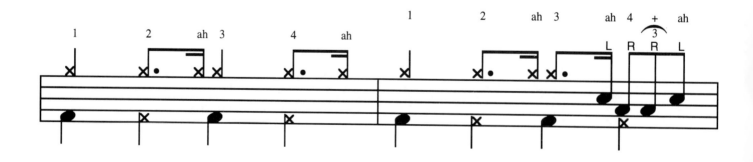

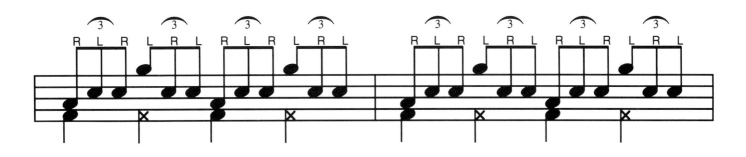

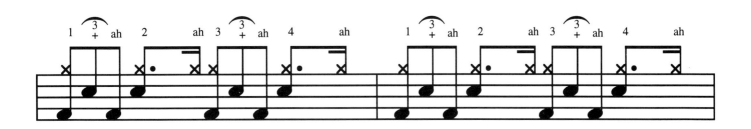

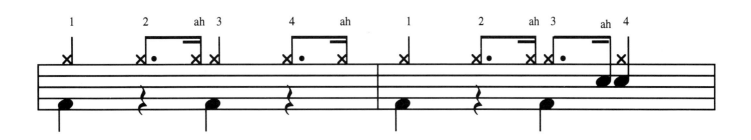

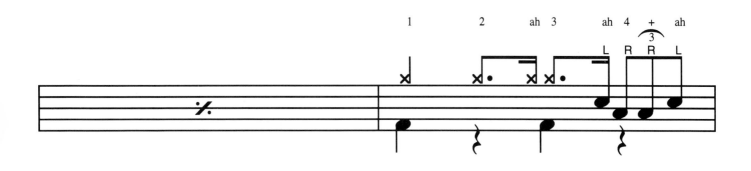

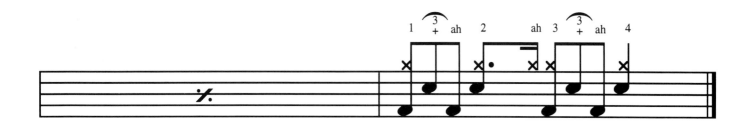

Solo No. 9

Jigsaw Jazz

This sixteen bar drum solo utilizes beats and fills with quarter notes, eighth and sixteenth notes from lessons 8 and 9. It is more important to place the emphasis on accuracy rather than speed. Try to create a relaxed flowing feel and allow the accents to highlight and colour the solo. Remember to count as you play along with the **"Beats Fills and Solos" C.D.**

131

Summary

Once you have completed this book, you will have aquired a good knowlege of how to play beats, fills and solos in a range of styles.

I hope you have found the grooves in this book easy to follow and helpful in developing your style and technique as a modern drummer.

For an introduction to basic drumming for the beginner see "Introducing Drums" by Steve Shier.
For great triplet and paradiddle studies see "Introducing All Around The Drums" by Steve Shier.
Please note that it is important to keep your drum kit sounding great. For correct tuning methods see "Introducing How To Tune The Drums" also by Steve Shier.